How to Wreck a Building

How to Wreck a Building

by Elinor Lander Horwitz

photographs by Joshua Horwitz

Pantheon Books

New York

The author and photographer wish to acknowledge the enthusiastic cooperation of Mahoney Brothers Company of Baltimore, Maryland, and Crouse Construction Company of Darlington, Maryland. We extend our specific thanks to George Mahoney, Jr., C. C. Crouse, Jr., and Gary Lee, as well as to Louis A. Franz, principal, and the faculty and students of Waverly School.

Library of Congress Cataloging in Publication Data

Horwitz, Elinor Lander.   How to wreck a building.
Summary: Chronicles the demolition of an old school.
1. Wrecking—Juvenile literature. [1. Wrecking]
I. Horwitz, Joshua, ill. II. Title.
TH153.H634 1982   690'.26   81-14185
ISBN 0-394-85155-2   AACR2
ISBN 0-394-95155-7 (lib. bdg.)

For N. H. H. and M. M.

I FELT REALLY SAD when I found out that my old school was going to be torn down. The building was seventy-one years old, and it's true it was getting pretty crackly, but there are plenty of buildings in the world a lot older and cracklier—like what about the pyramids in Egypt? No one's knocking them down.

Waverly Elementary School is the best place to go to school in Baltimore because it's right near Memorial Stadium, the home of the Baltimore Orioles. The new Waverly School—the one we moved into—was built next door to the old one.

The new school is low and square and plain. The old school was tall and fancy. It had two cupolas on the roof with round copper domes and points on top, like the spikes on old-time helmets.

One day just before the wreckers came, I was standing looking at the school. Somebody had already broken the windows of my old room. A man stopped to look too. He said, "A lot of memories are going to go with that school," and I agreed. I went there from kindergarten up to the middle of fifth grade, when we moved to the new school. I remember every room and all the places where certain things happened way back when I was a little kid.

The desks were banged up and the ceilings were tin and there were great big bathrooms in the basement. Near the street there was a stone monument to the graduates of Waverly School who died in World War I. I guess it was pretty old-fashioned— but I liked it a lot.

The day we left the old school I went into my sister's class to help pack books. She was writing all over the blackboard, "Good-bye school, I love you school," and dopey things like that. I laughed at her and she got mad. Of course my sister is only a third-grader.

Everyone was excited about moving into the new school. But when we filed out at the end of the day a lot of bigger kids waved and shouted, "Good-bye old school," and I was sorry I had laughed at my sister. Then the principal locked the door and said, "The school is officially closed." My teacher was crying. When she saw me looking at her, she put on her sunglasses. That's when I realized I'd never in my whole life be in that school again, not even to visit.

My father went to the old school too, when he was a kid. He said we were lucky to be getting a new school with all the modern facilities. He said the old school wasn't safe anymore. But then he shook his head and smiled and said, "No one puts up buildings like that nowadays. Those doors are solid oak. The hinges and doorknobs are solid brass. That curved staircase railing in front is solid cast iron. The stone-work is real old-time masonry."

I said, "If it's so solid, why don't they just leave it there?"

"Because it isn't safe anymore," my father said.

The day they started taking the school
down, our teacher said we were lucky
because we had watched the new school
being built and now we'd see the old
school being demolished. She said we
ought to take advantage of the opportunity
and try to learn all we could about how
they wreck a building.

I was still feeling pretty sad just
thinking about it—and then the action
began.

BANG!

It was the scrap metal men yanking out
radiators and throwing them into a truck.

13

On the way to school the next day, I saw a man from Mars going in one of the doors. Anyhow, that's what he looked like. He said he was there to take out all the asbestos around the furnace and the pipes. He said it's the law—asbestos is a hazardous material and it all has to come out and be buried in a special landfill before demolition can begin.

Other people came. They disconnected the lines and pipes that used to bring water, gas, and electricity to the school. They took away some of the big heavy old blackboards. The next day men were up on the roof removing slates so they could be used on another building. It was good to know that some parts of our old school wouldn't just be thrown away or melted down.

That afternoon three men put up a tall fence around the school. I asked them why they were doing it. "To keep out people like you, kid," they said.

The day the demolition began I ran over to the school very early. The crane was already there, and two men were attaching the clam bucket to the end of the boom. The crane operator said they call it a clam bucket because it opens and shuts like a clam.

I asked him why they didn't just burn the building down or blow it up with dynamite. He said that if they set it on fire most of it wouldn't burn, and if they dynamited it they'd weaken the foundations of all the houses across the street.

The first blow was struck on a rainy Monday morning at about eight o'clock. By the time I came out of school at three in the afternoon, places that had always been inside were outside. It was raining on the yellow walls of my second-grade classroom, and some of the kids' papers were still tacked to the wall. I knew it was necessary, but it sure didn't seem right.

Later that afternoon the crane operator whacked the building a few times with an iron wrecking ball. I found out that the ball weighs one and a half tons, but it didn't work on our school. The problem was that the brick was soft. The crane operator said a wrecking ball was fine for a concrete building, but on the bricks of our old school it was like hitting into a sponge. So he went back to using the clam bucket.

Actually, I don't think it looks like a clam. What it really looks like is an enormous hungry mouth with big strong teeth.

18

It can be used two ways. The first way is to grab and hold and pull at things.

It can also be used like a wrecking ball to bang against the building and break it up.

Here's one thing I learned right away.
Sometimes when people describe a loud
noise, they say it sounded like a building
falling down. Well, now I know what
they're talking about.

20

You could hear the old Waverly School
coming down as far away as the avenue.

21

You would have to say it wasn't a very peaceful scene, but it sure wasn't boring. Here are some of the sounds you could hear on the way over, even before you came around the corner:

The motor of the crane
The motors of the front-end loaders
    and dump trucks
The bucket smashing against the walls
Glass breaking
Bricks falling
Iron beams falling
Wood being crunched
Staircases collapsing
Ceilings falling in

Here's something I'd never thought about before. It took so many people to put the building up—bricklayers, stone-masons, carpenters, plumbers, electricians, plasterers, roofing people, floor layers, painters. It really takes just one person—the crane operator—to pull it all down.

The machine they used to take down our school is called a fifty-ton truck crane. The two main parts are the truck or crane carrier and the boom. The truck has twelve wheels; a cab in front, where someone sits to drive the truck to the job or move it around; and another cab in back called the house, which swivels on a turntable. The controls for the crane are inside the house. The crane operator sits in there and uses three foot pedals and five hand levers to move the crane up and down and from side to side, and to move the bucket and open and close it.

The boom they used was ninety feet high, but it can be extended to go as high as one hundred and sixty feet. Some cranes use diesel fuel, but this one ran on gasoline. It guzzled about sixty-five gallons during a work day.

The man who works with the crane operator is called the oiler. He drives the crane when they have to change its position. He fills it with gas from a tank on the truck. His most important job is to take care of the equipment, but he doesn't just oil it. When cables break he fixes them. When the bucket gets busted he fixes that. Because the crane is doing such heavy work all day long, it needs a lot of maintenance.

I watched the demolition every day. It was hard to watch the old school go, but it would have been a lot harder *not* to watch it.

Other people watched too. Kids from school watched, and people in the neighborhood stood at the fence or sat on the curb across the street.

There was always someone sitting on the monument.

Every day the building looked less like a school and more like a wreck.

For the first few days the crane was the only machine on the job, but soon there were dump trucks and front-end loaders. The loaders lifted the piles of bricks, stone, wood, plaster, pieces of tin ceiling, pieces of staircase, pieces of light fixtures, pieces of doors, gutters and drains, sinks and toilets and filled the dump trucks. All sorts of different things that were put into that building separately over seventy years ago came out all mixed up together.

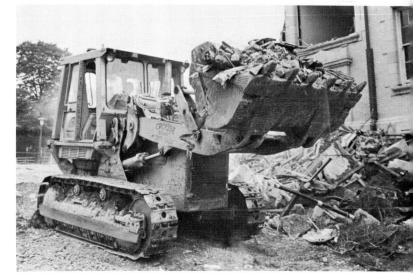

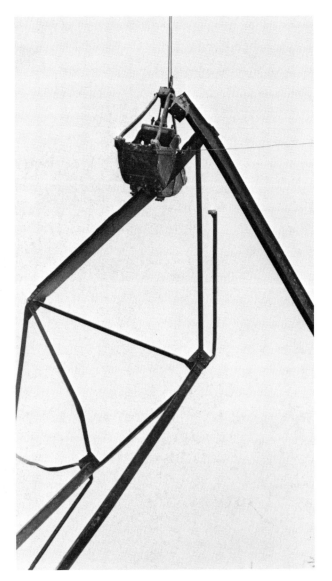

The roof copper and the pipes and iron beams were separated from the rest of the rubble to be sold to scrap metal companies. The crane would hand heavy iron beams and lead pipes to the loader, and the loader would hand them on to the truck that was waiting to take them away. The machines seemed to be working together as if they were people.

The loaders also battered away at the lower parts of the building while the crane attacked the high parts.

The oiler attached a big hose to a fire hydrant and sprayed water on the building and on the rubble heaps to keep the dust down.

It didn't do much good. Every time huge chunks of building came crashing down I felt like I was in the middle of a dust storm.

I ran to the school every day so I could be there at seven-thirty, when they started work. At lunchtime I walked over to see what had changed during the morning. After school I was back at the fence until the men left.

Sometimes my friends and I would talk about the good things we used to do in the old school. In the old school the windows were so tall you had to open them with a special stick. It was a big deal to be allowed to open the windows when we were in about the third or fourth grade.

In the old school the floors were wood and the steps were iron. You could make a lot of noise when you ran, and you could yell in the hall and get a great echo. The new school has vinyl tiles on the ceilings, and carpets. It's so quiet it doesn't seem like a real school.

36

In the old school you could look out the third-floor windows and see the whole city of Baltimore right to the Inner Harbor. The new school is downhill and low, and there isn't much to look at now that the demolition is finished. While they were working I had a ringside seat.

We also thought up ideas for how they could have made use of the school building after we moved out.

Teddy said since the bottom windows had bars, they could have used it for a jail, with maybe a cafeteria upstairs.

Quin said it was big enough to have been an apartment house.

Angela said they could have kept it as a haunted house to use for Halloween parties.

Rachel said maybe it could have been a place for teachers to stay. Her teacher lives in Annapolis and has to drive back and forth every day.

Gregory said the building was so strong it should have been used as a place for people to go to in a disaster.

Mark said there are a lot of poor people in Baltimore who don't have homes and could have stayed there.

Anyhow—by the time we got to talking about it, it would have taken about three years and a million dollars to build the old school back again. There was sky where the library used to be.

One morning when I arrived, the top of the school looked more like a bridge than a building. You could see through the whole big spooky attic I sneaked up into once when they left the hatch open.

The two cupolas were still standing on top of that rickety bridge. When they knocked off the first one I remembered how sad I had felt when I first heard that the building was coming down. It wasn't so hard seeing the second one go. It looked awful up there all alone.

After the cupolas came down you wouldn't have known—if you'd just passed by in a car—what kind of building had been there. Nothing you could recognize from the old school was left.

I thought the whole skinny skeleton would collapse in an hour, and I guess the crane operator had the same idea. He tugged and tugged at it with the bucket. He hit the iron with the wrecking ball.

There was plenty of noise but nothing happened.

At the end of the day a welder came and cut through each of the standing beams near the bottom with a blowtorch.

After that a special loader came that had a winch on the back. The oiler went up in the bucket and tied a cable around one of the beams, above the cut. Then, as the loader drove away toward the fence, the cable tightened and pulled and pulled...

44

and... WOW!!!

47

You might say I lost my past.

At least I lost my kindergarten room, my first-grade room, my second-grade room, my third-grade room, my fourth-grade room, and the room I had for half of fifth grade, plus the attic.

Don't think it isn't hard to lose your past, even if you *are* lucky to be in one of the first classes in a brand-new school.

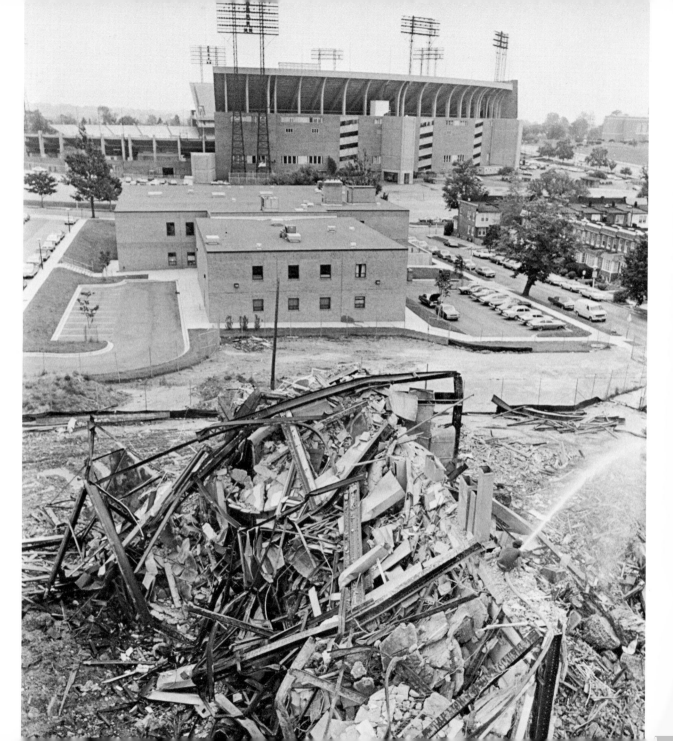

It really is too bad that the old school had to come down, but I have to admit that the demolition was the most exciting thing that ever happened in our neighborhood.

Before the demolition started, the principal told us how lucky we were because pretty soon we'd be playing baseball on the ground where the school used to stand. Most of the kids thought that was a great idea, but I thought it was weird. It just didn't seem right.

51

Actually, it turned out to be okay.

53

Here's what's left of the old school: the World War I monument, which is right where it's always been; and the old cornerstone, which the wreckers brought over to the new school for a souvenir.

Last week we had a cornerstone-laying ceremony. We looked at the old cornerstone. Then they put a new cornerstone into the wall of the new school. Inside was a metal box with pictures of every single student inside it.

I used to sit at my old desk and think about kids who were in that room seventy years ago. Maybe seventy years from now they'll tear down the new school and people will look at our pictures and wonder what we were like.

One of the boys in the class gave a talk about the history of our school. At the end he said, "The old building is now a thing of the past. Time moves on and so must we." My teacher clapped and said, "Well put," and she was smiling. I guess she's gotten over feeling so sad.

I guess I have too.

55

Elinor Lander Horwitz has been a freelance writer since 1963. She has written articles for newspapers and national magazines, three U.S. government publications on water quality, and over a dozen books for young readers. Ms. Horwitz collects American folk art, and designed a gargoyle that is now part of the National Cathedral. She and her husband, neurosurgeon Norman Horwitz, live in Chevy Chase, Maryland. They have three children.

Joshua Horwitz attended Princeton University and received a B.F.A. degree from the Institute of Film and Television at New York University. He recently visited southeast Asia, where he worked at a refugee camp in southern Thailand, and traveled through India and Nepal. Mr. Horwitz does free-lance work in film and video, and his photographs appear in three previous books by Elinor Lander Horwitz. He lives in New York City.